Kristi,

I often Lo... [illegible]
I didn't record the precious moments and thoughts as you were growing up. Perhaps, in this book, you can do that.

I love you,
Mom

_____

_____

_____

_____

_____

_____

_____

_____

_____

_____

_____

_____

_____

When God thought of mother,
He must have laughed with satisfaction,
and framed it quickly—
so rich, so deep, so divine,
so full of soul, power, and beauty,
was the conception.

Henry Ward Beecher

When a woman becomes a mother, right from the outset it becomes clear that the role is not quite as straightforward as perhaps she thought it was going to be.

_____

_____

_____

_____

_____

_____

_____

_____

_____

_____

_____

_____

_____

_____

_____

_____

_____

_____

The world is full of specialists and experts in everything conceivable, but what is a mother? She must be a nurse, carer, play leader, a teacher, a language tutor, a psychologist, guide, counselor, team coach, mentor, and companion.

Each mother is an artist and each of our children is an exquisite work of art.

Mothers provide shelter in stormy weather, refreshment in drought, shade in a heat wave, and a warm hearth in cold winters.

Knowing what it is to be a mother is the gateway
to knowing what it is to be human.

A mother's stories, like those of all great storytellers, are told from the heart—full of detail, color, and passion.

Oh what power is motherhood,
Possessing a potent spell.
All women alike
Fight fiercely for a child.

Euripides

All I am I owe to my mother. I attribute all my success in life to the moral, intellectual, and physical education I received from her.

George Washington

Every mother is a goddess to her children—a wonderful and wondrous goddess to be worshipped and adored.

God couldn't be everywhere so he created mothers.

The Talmud

Through mother's eyes our world seems
bigger, brighter, and happier.

Wherever there is a child performing in the school play, there is a mother prepared to sit up all night sewing a costume.

Show to me a woman who is loyal, constant, selfless, generous, steadfast, kind, loving, encouraging, strong, unshakable, dedicated, cunning, and wise—and I will show to you a mother.

Nothing can compare with a mother's sorrow
at being parted from her offspring.

Mothers mold, shape, and color their unique
creations, every day, in everything they do.

Wherever a child has a dark cloud hanging over his or her head there is to be found a mother capable of bringing out the sun again.

Mothers don't even think in terms of sacrifice. No matter what they give up to raise their children, it is always worth it.

At the flick of a switch in her child's imagination, a mother becomes not a parent but a sidekick in a two-man mission to Mars, a dragonfly, a fairy princess, or a friendly giant; she's a pop star, a professor, and a playmate.

Every mother carefully constructs a small, protected world
into which she first brings her child.

MQ Publications Ltd · 12 The Ivories · 6–8 Northampton Street · London N1 2HY
Tel: +44 (0)20 7359 2244 · Fax: +44 (0)20 7359 1616 · mail@mqpublications.com
www.mqpublications.com